JOHN RIGGS

Game On!

Level Up Your Teaching With Gamification

First edition

This book was professionally typeset on Reedsy.
Find out more at reedsy.com

"It is the supreme art of the teacher to awaken joy in creative expression and knowledge."

— Albert Einstein

Contents

Preface

Welcome, fellow educators, to "Game On: Level Up Your Teaching"! Prepare to embark on a journey that will revolutionize your approach to education and transform your classroom into an engaging, dynamic, and student-centered learning environment. Get ready to unlock the power of gamification and witness the incredible impact it can have on your students' enthusiasm, motivation, and academic achievement.

In this book, we will delve into the fascinating realm of gamification, where the principles of game design and mechanics merge with the art of teaching. Together, we will explore how to leverage the innate love for play and competition that resides within all of us to enhance the learning experience and empower our students to reach new heights.

Now, you might be wondering, what exactly is gamification? It's not about turning your classroom into a giant arcade or replacing textbooks with game consoles (though that does sound pretty fun, doesn't it?). Gamification is about harnessing the elements of games - the challenges, rewards, competition, and collaboration - and infusing them into our teaching practices to create an immersive and interactive learning environment.

Imagine a classroom where students are excited to learn, eagerly participating in activities, and taking ownership of their educational journey. Picture students fully engaged, their eyes gleaming with excitement as they conquer academic quests, earn badges, and level up their skills. That's the magic of gamification in action!

Throughout this book, we will uncover the secrets of successful gamification implementation, drawing from real-world examples, research-based strategies, and practical advice. You will discover how to gamify your lessons, design captivating quests and challenges, incorporate game mechanics into your assessments, and foster a positive classroom culture of collaboration and growth.

But let's not forget the most important part – having fun! We'll infuse humor, excitement, and a spirit of adventure into every chapter. After all, teaching should be enjoyable, and learning should be an exhilarating quest. So get ready to unleash your creativity, embrace the unexpected, and take risks as we embark on this gamified teaching adventure together. You'll quickly notice that I end each sub chapter with enthusiasm. That's by design – trying new things takes courage, and I'm here to cheer you on! You've got this!

Remember, as educators, we hold the power to shape young minds and ignite the spark of lifelong learning. By embracing the principles of gamification, we can tap into our students' natural curiosity, motivation, and competitive spirit, and transform our classrooms into vibrant hubs of discovery and growth.

So, fellow teachers, let's level up our teaching game and embark on this epic journey of gamification together. Are you ready? It's time to say, "Game On!"

1

What Is Gamified Learning?

Understanding the Concept of Gamification

In recent years, there has been a growing interest in the concept of utilizing gamelike aspects in education, which is commonly referred to as gamification. As educators, it is of utmost importance for us to delve into this innovative approach and its potential to effectively captivate students in our classrooms. This particular section strives to offer a comprehensive comprehension of gamifying learning and its capacity to inspire students through interactive and immersive learning encounters.

Gamification encompasses the integration of game elements and principles into non-game situations, such as education. By implementing concepts derived from game design, educators possess the capability to convert traditional learning activities into captivating experiences that seize the attention of students. The ultimate objective is to heighten student involvement, motivation, and learning outcomes.

An integral aspect entails the utilization of rewards and incentives, comparable to those encountered in games. Students are acknowledged and rewarded for their accomplishments, progress, and exertion. These rewards can assume various forms, such as points, badges, levels, or virtual currencies, which instill in students a sense of achievement and stimulate their ongoing participation. Furthermore, the introduction of leaderboards and elements of healthy competition can serve as additional sources of motivation for students' engagement.

Another substantial element entails the incorporation of narratives and storytelling. By constructing meaningful and relatable stories, educators can enhance the learning experience, making it more engaging. By placing students in roles which necessitate active participation and problem solving, they develop a sense of ownership regarding their progress and actively involve themselves in the learning process.

Moreover, gamification allows for personalized learning experiences. Through the utilization of adaptive learning platforms or game based learning applications, students can receive tailored content and challenges that align with their individual strengths, weaknesses, and progress. This customized approach not only cultivates a deeper understanding among students but also fosters a sense of autonomy and self-directed learning.

It is crucial to note that I am not proposing the replacement of traditional teaching methods with gamified learning, but rather the enhancement of these methods. Gamified learning can be seamlessly integrated into existing curricula and instructional strategies. By amalgamating gamification with other teaching approaches, educators can establish a dynamic and captivating learning environment that caters to various learning styles and preferences.

Comprehending gamification holds significant importance for educators striving to enhance student engagement and motivation. By incorporating game elements, rewards, narratives, and personalized learning experiences, gamified learning possesses the potential to revolutionize conventional classrooms into interactive and effective learning spaces. Embracing gamification in education permits us to tap into the inherent motivation and enthusiasm of students, thus nurturing a genuine passion for learning that extends beyond the confines of the classroom.

* * *

Benefits of Gamified Learning in the Classroom

"The incorporation of gamification into the realm of education has attracted considerable attention as an inventive means to captivate and enrich students' learning experiences. This section delves into the advantages of integrating gamification into the classroom, addressing the needs of teachers seeking to adopt this approach in their teaching methods.

One of the primary merits of gamification in education lies in its capacity to heighten student motivation and engagement. By harnessing students' inherent inclination towards games, educators can cultivate an interactive and dynamic learning environment that captures their attention and actively involves them in the learning process. This heightened engagement leads to increased participation, better retention of information, and an augmented enthusiasm for learning.

Furthermore, gamified learning nurtures a sense of autonomy and self directed learning. By incorporating game elements such as quests, challenges, and rewards, students are empowered to take control of their learning journey. They are endowed with the liberty to chart their own paths, set goals, and make decisions, thereby fostering a sense of responsibility and independence. This intrinsic motivation propels students to explore and unravel knowledge on their own, facilitating a deeper understanding of the subject matter.

In addition, gamification fosters collaboration and teamwork among students. Many gamified learning platforms offer opportunities for students to collaborate, working together to solve problems and achieve shared objectives. By cultivating a cooperative atmosphere, students develop critical skills such as communication, negotiation, and cooperation, all of which are indispensable for success in the contemporary world.

Moreover, gamified learning provides students with immediate feedback, enabling them to track their progress and adapt accordingly. Through interactive features like leaderboards, badges, and levels, students can effortlessly evaluate their performance and identify areas that require improvement. This instantaneous feedback not only motivates students but also instills a growth mindset and a willingness to take risks.

Lastly, gamification has the potential to render complex concepts more accessible and enjoyable. By presenting information in a gamified format, abstract ideas can be transformed into interactive and relatable experiences. This approach caters to diverse learning styles and encourages a profound comprehension of the subject matter.

As can be observed, gamified learning yields numerous advantages for educators endeavoring to cultivate an interactive and dynamic learning environment for their students. By harnessing the power of gamification, educators can bolster student motivation, foster autonomy and collaboration, provide timely feedback, and create an enjoyable learning experience. The integration of gamified learning in the classroom possesses the potential to revolutionize education and equip students for success in the contemporary world.

* * *

Challenges and Concerns

Educators are actively exploring novel approaches to captivate their students. By integrating game aspects into the classroom setting, teachers can tap into the innate motivation and pleasure derived from playing games. However, there exist numerous challenges and considerations linked to the implementation of gamification that educators should be mindful of.

One primary challenge pertains to the substantial time and effort demanded for the planning and development process. Designing a gamified curriculum requires the creation of a framework, the establishment of goals, and the mapping out of specific game elements to be utilized. Teachers must also navigate through the technical aspects, which entail selecting suitable digital tools or platforms to facilitate the gamified experience. Given the already arduous workload, this process can be time consuming and demanding.

Another concern involves ensuring the alignment of gamified learning with the curriculum and learning objectives. While the integration of game elements can enhance engagement, it is imperative to find a balance between entertainment and educational content. Teachers must guarantee that the game elements contribute to the learning experience rather than divert attention from it. This necessitates meticulous planning and continuous evaluation to ensure that the gamified activities are in line with the desired learning outcomes.

Acquiring student buy-in poses yet another challenge that teachers may encounter when introducing gamification. Some students may resist or dismiss gamified learning as "childish" or not academically rigorous enough. It is vital for educators to address these concerns and emphasize the educational benefits. By effectively communicating the purpose and relevance of gamified learning, teachers can assist students in recognizing its value and fostering their active participation.

Furthermore, the integration of technology can be intimidating for teachers who may lack familiarity or comfort with digital tools. Teachers require sufficient training and support to effectively utilize the necessary technology. This includes troubleshooting any technical issues that may arise during the implementation process.

While the gamification of learning holds promise for engaging students, it is crucial for teachers to acknowledge and address the associated challenges. These challenges encompass the time and effort required for planning and development, ensuring alignment with the curriculum and learning objectives, gaining student buy-in, and effectively integrating technology. By proactively tackling these challenges, teachers can leverage the power of gamified learning to create a dynamic and captivating classroom environment.

2

Getting Started with Gamification

Setting Clear Learning Objectives

When it comes to gamified learning, one thing we can't overlook is the importance of clear and actionable learning objectives. As educators, it's crucial for us to establish precise goals that provide both students and ourselves with guidance throughout the learning process. In this section, we'll dive into why clear learning objectives are so significant in the context of gamification, and we'll also share some practical strategies to engage students and enrich their learning experience.

Now, gamification of learning is all about infusing game elements into the classroom to spark active participation, intrinsic motivation, and that satisfying sense of accomplishment. But here's the thing: without clear learning objectives, those game elements can easily turn into distractions that hinder students' progress. By setting clear objectives, teachers can ensure that game mechanics align with educational goals, so that every element of the game contributes to student learning.

Let's start with how clear learning objectives benefit students. These objectives act as a roadmap for their learning journey. When objectives are spelled out clearly, students know exactly what's expected of them and can keep track of their progress. This clarity empowers them to take ownership of their learning, fostering a sense of agency and self-directedness.

But it's not just students who benefit from clear learning objectives; teachers do too. These objectives serve as a compass, guiding teachers in designing gamified activities that align with specific learning outcomes. Teachers can identify the game mechanics and elements that best support the achievement of these objectives, creating meaningful engagement and enhancing student learning.

To establish clear learning objectives, we need to consider the specific content and skills that we want to address. We should aim for objectives that are specific, measurable, attainable, relevant, and time-bound (yes, they're SMART!). This framework ensures that our objectives are realistic and achievable, while also challenging students to grow.

Now, it's not enough to have SMART objectives; we also need to effectively communicate them to our students. Clearly articulating the learning objectives at the beginning of a gamified unit or lesson gives students a clear sense of purpose and direction. We can use visual aids like charts or posters to prominently display the objectives in the classroom, serving as constant reminders that motivate students to strive for their goals.

Ultimately, clear learning objectives are the foundation of gamified learning. By defining specific goals, teachers can align game elements with educational outcomes, enabling students to embrace purpose and direction. Clear objectives empower students to take charge of their learning, while also guiding teachers in designing engaging and effective gamified activities. By thoughtfully integrating game mechanics, teachers can create an immersive and transformative learning experience for students.

Remember, gamified learning is like adding a sprinkle of magic to education. Embrace the power of clear learning objectives and embark on an exciting journey of gamified learning!

* * *

Choosing the Right Game Elements for Your Classroom

Education can be a bit of a maze, but thankfully, gamification has emerged as a fantastic strategy to captivate students and make learning a whole lot more exciting. By infusing game elements into the classroom, teachers can create an interactive environment that gets students actively involved. But here's the secret sauce: you need to carefully choose the right game elements that align with your teaching goals and objectives.

Step one on this gamification journey is figuring out what you want your students to achieve. Are you aiming to boost their critical thinking, encourage collaboration, or unleash their inner creativity? Once you've got a clear picture of your objectives, it's time to pick the game elements that will help you achieve those goals.

One nifty game element you can introduce is points and rewards. By assigning points for completing tasks or mastering concepts, you're giving your students a little taste of the sweet nectar of motivation. And hey, those points can be cashed in for rewards like privileges or good old-fashioned recognition. Not only does this get them actively participating, but it also reinforces positive behavior and the effort they put in.

Next up on the game element menu is good old competition. Injecting some friendly rivalry into the classroom can really spice things up. Leaderboards displaying students' progress and achievements can create a buzz of excitement and engagement. You see, humans have this innate drive to outshine their peers, so competition can inspire your students to go that extra mile and achieve academic greatness.

Collaboration is a game element that shouldn't be overlooked. By throwing in some group activities or team-based challenges, you're giving your students the chance to work together, communicate like pros, and sharpen their problem-solving skills. It's like building a tight-knit squad in the classroom, fostering a sense of camaraderie and creating a supportive community.

Oh, and let's not forget about personalization. Each student is a unique individual with their own set of strengths and interests. By letting them choose their learning path or customize their avatars, you're handing them the reins and letting them take control of their own learning adventure. Talk about empowerment!

Brace yourself, because when you implement gamification in the classroom, magical things can happen. But remember, you've got to choose the right game elements that align with your teaching goals. Mix it up with a winning combination of points and rewards, healthy competition, collaboration, and personalization, and you'll create a learning environment that's not only interactive and immersive but also super engaging and set for academic success.

Now, go forth and gamify like a boss!

* * *

Creating a Game-Based Curriculum

Let's dive into the exciting realm of creating a curriculum that brings the magic of games into the classroom! In this section, we'll explore practical strategies and insights for all you teachers out there who are eager to embark on the journey of gamified learning.

The first step in developing a game-based curriculum is to establish clear learning objectives. We want to make sure that game mechanics and content align with our educational goals, so the game becomes an effective instructional tool instead of a mere distraction. This means pinpointing the essential concepts and skills that our students need to master and designing game elements that reinforce and assess these learning outcomes.

Once we've got our objectives in place, it's time to select the right game mechanics and structures that support those goals. We can consider elements like points, levels, badges, and leaderboards to create a sense of healthy competition and achievement. It's also important to strike a balance between individual and collaborative game play and integrate feedback and assessment mechanisms that promote continuous improvement.

Creating a game-based curriculum requires some serious planning and design skills. We need to carefully plan the progression of challenges, making sure they become progressively more complex and scaffolded to support student growth. And hey, let's not forget about the game's narrative and theme! These elements can really amp up student engagement and immerse them in the learning process.

Implementing a game-based curriculum calls for a supportive classroom environment. We need to clearly communicate expectations and rules while also giving our students a sense of autonomy and agency within the game. This helps cultivate a positive and collaborative culture where students feel motivated and empowered to take charge of their own learning. It's all about creating that perfect blend of structure and freedom.

Last but not least, ongoing assessment and reflection are essential parts of a game-based curriculum. We need to regularly evaluate how effective our game elements are in achieving the desired learning outcomes. And guess what? Feedback from our students is gold! By gathering their input and adapting the game as needed, we keep it dynamic and relevant, ensuring it remains a powerful learning tool.

So, my fellow educators, let's embrace the power of gamification in learning! By tapping into the intrinsic motivation and engagement that games offer, we can transform our classrooms into interactive and immersive learning experiences. This journey will ultimately foster deeper understanding and long-lasting retention of key concepts and skills.

Are you ready to level up? Let the gamified learning adventure begin!

3

Designing Engaging Game-Based Lessons

Incorporating Gamified Elements in Lesson Planning

Let's dive into the exciting world of incorporating gamified elements into our lesson planning! As educators, we're always on the lookout for innovative teaching methods that can truly captivate and motivate our students. In this section, we'll explore how we can infuse our lesson plans with game–inspired elements to create an interactive and immersive learning environment that boosts student engagement and motivation.

One strategy that works like a charm is introducing rewards and incentives inspired by games. You know, those points, badges, and levels that students can earn as they make progress in their learning. These rewards not only acknowledge their achievements but also give them a delightful sense of fulfillment, inspiring them to keep pushing forward on their educational journey.

Another approach is to spice things up with challenges or quests that resemble games. By framing your learning objectives as exciting missions, you're making the content more relatable and enjoyable for your students. Imagine them stepping into the shoes of detectives, unraveling historical mysteries by examining evidence and making connections. Talk about an adventure!

But we can't forget the power of interactive technology tools. We can leverage online platforms that offer interactive quizzes or educational games, seamlessly integrating them into our lesson plans. These tools not only encourage active participation but also reinforce our learning objectives. Students can learn at their own pace, receiving immediate feedback that boosts their comprehension and retention of the material. It's like turning learning into a thrilling game!

Now, it's important to remember that gamification should never overshadow substantive learning. It's a tool that enhances the learning process, not replaces it. That's why it's crucial to align our gamified elements with our curriculum objectives and learning outcomes. We're creating a harmonious blend of fun and educational goodness.

Incorporating gamified elements into our lesson planning calls for creativity, adaptability, and a willingness to experiment. It's about embracing a fresh approach that transforms our classrooms into engaging and dynamic environments, where the flame of passion for learning burns bright. So, let's seize the potential of gamified learning as educators and embark on a journey that revolutionizes education, empowering our students to unleash their full potential.

Get ready for an adventure like no other! Game on!

* * *

Strategies for Effective Game-Based Instruction

Let's dive into the exciting world of game-based instruction, where education meets fun! In today's modern era, incorporating game elements in teaching has become a captivating and innovative method. By infusing our lessons with game-like aspects, we can truly engage our students and take their learning experiences to a whole new level. In this section, we'll explore some practical strategies that will help us make the most of this approach.

First things first, we need to establish clear learning objectives. Before we dive into the games, let's make sure that the content and mechanics align perfectly with our curriculum standards. We want to create meaningful learning experiences that hit the nail on the head.

When selecting games, choose ones that are suitable for your subject matter and the age group of your students. Look for games that offer educational value, promote critical thinking, and provide opportunities for collaboration and problem-solving. It's all about finding the right game for the right lesson.

Now, it's important to support our students throughout their game-based journey. Before jumping into the game play, offer them the necessary background knowledge and skills to succeed. Provide pre-game activities, tutorials, or brief lessons to prepare them and ensure they grasp the concepts we're teaching.

Reflection and feedback are key players in this game. Encourage your students to reflect on their game play experiences and connect them to the learning objectives. Offer constructive feedback to guide their progress and help them grow.

Teamwork makes the dream work! Games can be fantastic tools for promoting collaboration. Incorporate cooperative game play or group challenges that require students to work together, solve problems, make decisions, and achieve shared goals. It's all about fostering that team spirit.

Don't forget the power of gamification mechanics! Alongside the games themselves, utilize mechanics like points, badges, leaderboards, and level progression. These little tricks motivate and engage students, providing instant feedback, healthy competition, and a satisfying sense of achievement.

Balance is key! Find that sweet spot between challenge and enjoyment in the games you choose. Make sure the difficulty level suits your students, offering them a sense of accomplishment when they conquer obstacles, all while keeping the game play engaging and enjoyable.

Assess, assess, assess! Integrate both formative and summative assessments throughout your game-based instruction. Use quizzes, discussions, or written reflections to evaluate your students' understanding and progress. It's all about checking in and providing the guidance they need.

By implementing these strategies, we can tap into the true potential of gamification and create a stimulating and effective learning environment. Game-based instruction motivates our students, enhances their critical thinking skills, promotes collaboration, and helps them develop a deep understanding of the subject matter. So let's embrace this approach and revolutionize education, equipping our students with the skills they need to conquer the digital world of the 21st century.

Ready to play and learn? Let the games begin!

* * *

Adapting Traditional Lessons into Gamified Activities

Education is constantly evolving, and it's crucial for us teachers to find creative methods that capture our students' attention and contribute to their success. One approach that's gaining popularity is gamified learning. It's all about harnessing the power of games to take the learning experience to a whole new level. In this section, we'll dive into the concept of adapting traditional lessons into gamified activities, giving you some practical strategies to sprinkle some gamification magic in your classroom.

Traditional lessons can sometimes feel a bit, well, linear. Students passively absorb information from textbooks and lectures, and it's easy for their attention to drift away. But fear not! Gamified learning is here to save the day. By transforming your lessons into gamified activities, you'll create an engaging and interactive experience that grabs your students' attention and motivates them to actively participate.

The first step in this gamification journey is identifying your core learning objectives. We don't want to just slap on some game elements and call it a day. No, no. Gamification should go hand in hand with educational content. By aligning game mechanics with specific learning outcomes, you'll ensure that your students not only have a blast but also develop a deep understanding of the subject matter.

Now, let's talk about game elements. Points, levels, and achievements, oh my! These can be game-changers in tracking your students' progress and giving them a satisfying sense of accomplishment. Imagine turning a history lesson into a thrilling trivia game, where students earn points for correct answers and unlock new levels as they advance. It's excitement and healthy competition rolled into one.

Get ready to unleash your storytelling prowess. By weaving a compelling narrative into your lessons, you'll create an emotional connection that makes the learning experience more memorable. Picture a science lesson on the solar system transforming into an interactive adventure, where students explore planets, solve puzzles, and work together to save the galaxy. It's like stepping into their very own sci-fi movie!

To ensure the success of your gamified activities, clear instructions and a supportive learning environment are key. Communicate the rules and objectives of the game with crystal clarity, and provide continuous feedback and guidance to your students. Remember to embrace flexibility and adaptability, as students may progress at different paces. We're all in this game together!

Adapting traditional lessons into gamified activities is a surefire way to engage your students and elevate their learning experiences. By incorporating game elements, storytelling, and clear objectives, you'll create a dynamic and interactive classroom environment that ignites curiosity, motivation, and deep understanding. Embracing gamification is like giving education a turbo boost, equipping your students with the skills they need to conquer the 21st century with confidence.

Let's level up our teaching game and make learning an epic adventure!

4

Utilizing Technology in Gamified Learning

Selecting Appropriate Digital Tools for Gamified Learning

In the vast landscape of digital tools and platforms available today, choosing the right ones for gamification can seem like navigating a maze. This sub chapter will guide you through the process of selecting the perfect digital tools that will elevate your gamified learning experience to new heights!

Define Your Objectives

Before diving headfirst into the sea of options, take a moment to clarify your goals and objectives. What specific learning outcomes do you want to achieve through gamification? Do you want to improve collaboration, reinforce content knowledge, or enhance critical thinking skills? Having a clear understanding of your objectives will help you make informed decisions when selecting digital tools.

Consider Student Preferences

Remember, the heart and soul of gamification are the students themselves. Take into account their preferences, interests, and technological capabilities. Are they more inclined towards competitive games or collaborative activities? Are they comfortable using specific devices or platforms? By considering student preferences, you'll ensure that the digital tools you choose resonate with them and spark their enthusiasm.

Research, Research, Research

Once you have a solid grasp of your objectives and student preferences, it's time to dive into the realm of research. Explore different websites, platforms, and apps that align with your goals. Read reviews, seek recommendations from fellow educators, and even test out the tools yourself. Remember, knowledge is power, and the more you know about a digital tool, the better equipped you'll be to make an informed decision.

Seek Compatibility

As you explore various digital tools, consider their compatibility with your existing classroom infrastructure. Will the tool integrate smoothly with your learning management system or other educational platforms you use? Does it require additional devices or software? Ensuring compatibility will save you from potential headaches and allow for a seamless integration of gamification into your classroom.

Trial and Error

Just like in the world of gaming, trial and error is key. Don't be afraid to experiment with different digital tools and platforms. Start with a small pilot project or use a tool for a specific activity to gauge its effectiveness. Pay attention to student feedback and adjust accordingly. Remember, it's all part of the learning process, and through trial and error, you'll discover the digital tools that work best for you and your students.

Embrace the Power of Community

The beauty of being an educator in the digital age is the wealth of knowledge and support available within the education community. Connect with fellow teachers, attend professional development workshops, or join online communities dedicated to gamification. By tapping into the collective wisdom and experiences of others, you'll uncover hidden gems and receive valuable insights on selecting the right digital tools.

In the end, selecting appropriate digital tools for gamification is a journey of exploration and discovery. By defining your objectives, considering student preferences, conducting thorough research, seeking compatibility, embracing trial and error, and leveraging the power of community, you'll embark on a path that leads to gamified learning experiences that truly engage and inspire your students. So, gear up, my fellow gamification enthusiasts, and let the quest for the perfect digital tools begin!

* * *

Integrating Gamification with Learning Management Systems

Let's dive into the exciting world of integrating gamification with learning management systems (LMS)! Gamification is all about bringing game elements and mechanics into non-game contexts to boost learner engagement and motivation. And you know what? LMS platforms like Google Classroom and others are the perfect playgrounds for this adventure. They're widely used by teachers for content delivery and student progress tracking. So, let's explore some practical ways to seamlessly incorporate gamification into LMS platforms and transform how students interact with educational content.

One key aspect of gamification in LMS is the implementation of badges, points, and leaderboards. Think of it as giving your students virtual medals, points, and a stage to show off their achievements. Awarding badges for task completion or reaching learning milestones taps into their desire for recognition and achievement. And hey, let's assign points for correct answers or timely assignment submissions to motivate active participation and excellence. It's like turning learning into a thrilling game show! Oh, and don't forget about leaderboards. They add that extra spice of healthy competition as students aim for the top positions. Who doesn't love a little friendly rivalry?

Get ready for quests and missions. Forget about those traditional assignments and quizzes. We're talking about designing quests that require students to embark on a series of exciting tasks and challenges. By framing learning objectives as quests, you're immersing your students in an epic learning adventure. It's like unleashing their inner heroes! And guess what? Successful quest completion can unlock additional content or rewards, making their journey even more thrilling. Talk about motivation boosters!

Let's not overlook the power of storytelling. You know how stories capture our imaginations and transport us to different worlds? Well, teachers can create narratives or scenarios that contextualize the learning material, turning it into a captivating adventure. By immersing students in a story line, you make learning more relatable and memorable. It's like giving education a plot twist that leaves a lasting impact. Better comprehension and retention? Check!

Integrating gamification with learning management systems opens up incredible opportunities for teachers to engage and motivate their students. By incorporating badges, points, leaderboards, quests, and storytelling, LMS platforms can evolve into immersive learning environments that capture students' attention and ignite a true passion for learning. So, let's harness the power of gamification, revolutionize content delivery, and create an enjoyable learning experience that leads to improved academic outcomes.

Ready to level up your teaching game? Let's dive into the world of gamified learning with our LMS platforms and make education an epic adventure!

* * *

Assessing Student Progress with Gamified Technology

In today's digital era, technology has become an integral part of our lives, and education is no exception. As teachers, it's crucial for us to adapt to the ever-changing educational landscape and embrace innovative methods that truly engage and motivate our students, leading to improved learning outcomes.

One approach that has gained popularity is gamified learning, which harnesses the power of games to foster intrinsic motivation, collaboration, and critical thinking skills among students. However, as educators, we need to recognize the importance of assessing student progress within this new learning environment. Luckily, gamified technology offers a wide range of assessment tools and strategies that can help us effectively evaluate student learning.

One of the great advantages of gamified technology is its ability to provide real-time feedback to both students and teachers. Through interactive quizzes, simulations, and game-based assignments, students receive immediate feedback on their performance, enabling them to identify their strengths and areas that need improvement. As teachers, we can use this feedback to tailor our instruction and provide targeted support to students who may benefit from it the most.

Another benefit of gamified technology is its capacity to track and analyze student data. By using learning management systems and game-based platforms, we can gather valuable insights into student progress, such as time spent on tasks, levels completed, and mastery of specific concepts. This data informs our instructional decisions, allowing us to design personalized learning paths for our students and effectively address their individual needs.

Furthermore, gamified technology empowers us to create authentic and engaging assessments that go beyond traditional paper-and-pencil tests. We can design quests, challenges, and simulations that require students to apply their knowledge and skills in real-world contexts. These assessments not only evaluate students' understanding but also cultivate higher-order thinking skills, problem-solving abilities, and creativity.

However, it's important to remember that while gamified technology offers valuable assessment opportunities, it shouldn't replace the formative and summative assessments we already use. Instead, it should be seen as a complementary tool that enhances our existing assessment practices.

Assessing student progress within the gamified learning environment is essential to ensure effective learning outcomes. Gamified technology provides diverse assessment tools and strategies that offer real-time feedback, track student data, and facilitate authentic assessments. By harnessing these tools, we can create a dynamic and engaging learning experience for our students, enhancing their motivation, collaboration, and critical thinking skills. As teachers, it's imperative that we embrace gamified technology and harness its potential to assess student progress effectively, ultimately promoting meaningful learning experiences.

5

Fostering Collaboration and Competition in the Classroom

Promoting Cooperative Learning through Gamification

Let's dive into the exciting world of promoting cooperative learning through gamification! Cooperative learning has long been recognized for its ability to boost student engagement, critical thinking skills, and academic performance. It creates a positive classroom environment that fosters collaboration, communication, and problem-solving. But hey, we all know implementing cooperative learning strategies can be a bit challenging, especially in schools. That's where gamification comes in, stealing the spotlight for good reason. It has the power to turn traditional learning experiences into immersive and interactive adventures. By integrating gamified elements into cooperative learning activities, teachers can cultivate an environment that ignites students' motivation to work together, learn from one another, and achieve shared objectives.

One effective approach to promote cooperative learning is by introducing team-based challenges and quests. These activities are designed to encourage collaboration, communication, and knowledge-sharing among students within their teams. By setting clear objectives, offering meaningful rewards, and fostering a healthy sense of competition, teachers can create an atmosphere of excitement and engagement in the classroom. It's like turning learning into an epic quest where students join forces to conquer challenges!

Another strategy is to utilize gamified assessment tools that allow students to demonstrate their understanding of the material while working cooperatively. Picture this: online quizzes with leaderboard features or interactive puzzles that require teamwork to solve. By incorporating elements of competition and cooperation, these assessments not only motivate students to actively participate but also provide opportunities for peer learning and support. Learning becomes a team sport!

Furthermore, gamification can be a game-changer in establishing a sense of achievement and progress within cooperative learning experiences. Implementing a leveling system or a point-based reward system enables students to track their individual and team progress. It's like unlocking new levels in a video game! This not only encourages healthy competition but also instills a sense of responsibility and accountability among students to contribute to their team's success.

When done right, gamification serves as a powerful tool to promote and sustain cooperative learning in classrooms. By incorporating game elements and mechanics into cooperative learning activities, teachers create an engaging and motivating environment where students collaborate, communicate, and learn from one another. From team-based challenges and quests to gamified assessment tools, the possibilities are endless. So, let's embrace the magic of gamification in learning and witness the thriving of our students! Together, we can make cooperative learning an epic adventure!

* * *

Implementing Team-Based Challenges and Quests

In the exciting world of education, it's crucial to find innovative and captivating approaches to ignite students' curiosity and foster a genuine passion for learning. By infusing the classroom with game elements, educators can create an immersive and interactive environment that sparks students' active engagement in their educational journey.

One powerful method for implementing gamified learning is the introduction of team-based challenges and quests. These activities not only promote collaboration and teamwork but also provide students with an opportunity to apply their knowledge and skills in practical and meaningful ways.

Team-based challenges and quests can take many forms, ranging from solving intricate puzzles and riddles to completing real-life simulations and projects. By dividing students into teams, educators foster a healthy spirit of competition that motivates students to collaborate, share ideas, and support each other in achieving a common goal.

These challenges can be thoughtfully designed to align with specific learning goals and curriculum standards, ensuring that students derive both enjoyment and essential knowledge and skills. For example, in a history class, students might embark on a quest to research and present a comprehensive timeline of significant events. In a science class, they could take on a challenge that requires designing and constructing a functional model to demonstrate a scientific principle.

To ensure the success of team-based challenges and quests, it's essential to provide clear instructions, establish transparent criteria for success, and set realistic goals. Educators should also actively monitor and provide feedback to the teams throughout the process, encouraging reflection and continuous improvement.

Furthermore, creating a supportive and inclusive environment where every student feels valued and included is paramount. Team-based challenges and quests offer an excellent opportunity to foster a sense of belonging as students learn to appreciate and leverage the unique strengths and perspectives of their teammates.

The incorporation of team-based challenges and quests represents a powerful approach to engage students through the magic of gamified learning. By integrating game-like elements into the classroom, educators can cultivate an environment that nurtures collaboration, critical thinking, problem-solving, and creativity. These activities not only make the learning experience more enjoyable but also equip students with essential skills for success in the 21st century. So, let the adventures begin, and get ready to witness your students thrive!

* * *

Harnessing the Power of Competition to Enhance Learning

Competition has always been a wild beast that can light up the fire of motivation in various aspects of life, and education is no exception. When it comes to gamified learning, competition takes on a whole new level of awesomeness. By infusing the learning process with competitive elements, educators can create an environment that ignites active participation, collaboration, and an insatiable hunger for improvement.

One of the best things about competition in gamified learning is its ability to tap into students' innate craving for challenge and achievement. When students are presented with clear goals to conquer, like earning points, badges, or leveling up, their desire to conquer those challenges goes through the roof. This inner motivation becomes a turbo boost that propels them to put in more effort and conquer any obstacles in their way.

Competition also fuels collaboration among students. By forming teams or setting up leaderboards, educators can foster peer-to-peer interaction and teamwork. Students get to join forces, brainstorm ideas, and support each other's learning journeys. This not only amplifies their understanding of the subject matter but also hones their superpowers of social skills and the ability to work as part of an unstoppable team.

And here's the cherry on top: competition serves up instant feedback to students on their progress and performance. With real-time scoring or ranking systems, students can gauge their own superhero abilities and compare them with those of their classmates. This feedback loop gives them the power to identify their strengths and weaknesses, making it possible to swoop in with targeted action to level up their skills.

To make the most of competition in gamified learning, educators need to strike the perfect balance. While a healthy dose of competition can spark student engagement like lightning bolts, going overboard and obsessing about winning can turn the fun into stress and anxiety. So, it's crucial to create a supportive and inclusive learning universe where every student feels like a superhero, empowered and motivated to conquer any challenge that comes their way.

Competition is a superpower in the realm of gamified learning, capable of unleashing student engagement and motivation like a lightning storm. By incorporating elements of competition, such as points, badges, and leaderboards, educators can tap into students' natural hunger for challenge and achievement. Competition fuels collaboration, dishes out immediate feedback, and shapes essential social skills. But remember, balance is key. Creating a supportive learning space where all students can unleash their inner superheroes is what truly makes gamified learning a mind-blowing experience. So, let the games begin and watch your students rise to the occasion, ready to conquer the challenges of the real world with gusto!

6

Assessing and Evaluating Gamified Learning

The Art of Assessing: Formative and Summative Strategies

Assessment is the secret sauce that spices up the learning process. It gives teachers the power to gauge student progress, pinpoint areas for improvement, and dish out timely feedback. When it comes to gamifying lessons, assessment becomes even more crucial. It helps us measure the impact of gamification on student engagement and achievement. So, let's dive into the world of assessment strategies, both ongoing and final, that can take our gamified learning to the next level.

First up, we have formative assessment, the cool cousin of assessments. It's all about gathering continuous feedback along the learning journey. Within the world of gamified learning, formative assessment seamlessly blends with game play. Think in-game quizzes, puzzles, or challenges that slyly assess students' understanding of the content. These assessments can even adapt to each student's performance, delivering personalized feedback and guidance. Talk about a tailor-made learning experience!

Now, let's talk about badges and achievements—the superheroes of formative assessment. As students power through the game, they earn badges and unlock achievements based on their mastery of skills and knowledge. These badges not only boost motivation but also serve as shiny proof of progress. By checking out the badges earned by each student, teachers get a glimpse into their strengths and areas for growth. It's like collecting superpowers!

Moving on to the grand finale, we have summative assessment, the ultimate showdown. This happens at the end of a unit or course to evaluate overall mastery. In the world of gamified learning, summative assessment gets a makeover. Picture a final challenge that students conquer or a culmination of epic tasks that showcase their learning. It's not just an assessment, it's a thrilling adventure where students can shine and celebrate their achievements.

And there's one more trick up our sleeves—portfolios! Students can create digital portfolios that showcase their gamified learning journey. These portfolios become a treasure trove of achievements, reflections, and evidence of growth. Sharing these portfolios with teachers and peers creates a full-circle view of students' progress and growth. It's like showcasing their skills on a virtual red carpet!

Formative and summative assessment strategies are the secret weapons of gamified learning. By seamlessly blending assessments into game play and unleashing the power of badges, achievements, quizzes, and portfolios, teachers can measure student progress, deliver timely feedback, and evaluate the success of gamified learning. It's a dynamic and engaging learning environment where students are motivated, collaborate, and achieve greatness. So, let's rock these assessments and make gamified learning a legendary adventure!

* * *

Unveiling the Secrets of Student Progress: Tracking and Analyzing Like a Pro

In the exciting realm of gamified learning, keeping tabs on student progress is like having a secret superpower. As educators, understanding how our students are doing is crucial for delivering effective instruction and personalizing their learning experience. So, let's dive into the world of tracking and evaluating student progress within a gamified learning environment and discover the tools and methods that make it all possible.

One nifty approach to track student progress is through the power of data analysis. By collecting and analyzing data on student performance, we unlock valuable insights into their strengths and weaknesses. This insight empowers us to tailor our instruction and support to meet their individual needs. Gamified learning platforms often come equipped with built-in analytics tools that give us the lowdown on student progress, from completion rates and scores to time spent on different tasks or levels. It's like having a treasure map to guide us to areas where students may need some extra help.

But that's not all! We also have the magical world of digital badges and achievements. In the gamified learning kingdom, students earn badges and achievements as they conquer challenges and make progress. These badges become visual representations of their mastery in various skills and knowledge areas. Best of all, they serve as little beacons of motivation, guiding students forward on their learning journey. And for us, educators, they become powerful tracking tools that allow us to see just how far our students have come.

Gamified learning platforms often offer features that provide real-time feedback and assessment. Through interactive quizzes, mini-games, and simulations, students get instant feedback on their performance. It's like having a personal coach cheering them on and guiding their next moves. And for us, educators, this real-time feedback is pure gold. It helps us spot any misconceptions or gaps in understanding and intervene with lightning speed.

And here's the grand finale: tracking and analyzing student progress can reveal fascinating trends and patterns in the learning process. By diving into the data on student engagement, participation, and performance, we unlock the secrets of what works best for our students in the gamified learning realm. Armed with this knowledge, we can make informed instructional decisions and continuously improve our gamified learning environment. It's like being a detective, solving the mystery of how to create the most engaging and effective learning experience.

Tracking and analyzing student progress are the secret weapons of gamified learning. With data analytics, digital badges, real-time feedback, and assessment tools in our arsenal, we gain valuable insights into student performance and can tailor our instruction to their unique needs. It's like crafting a personalized adventure for each student, guiding them towards success. So, let's embrace the power of tracking and analysis in gamified learning and unlock a world of personalized, engaging, and transformative education!

* * *

Unleashing the Power of Gamified Learning: Assessing Its Impact

Ah, gamified learning, the cool kid on the education block, bringing a whole new level of engagement and interactivity to the classroom. But hey, let's not just ride the trend wave without understanding its true impact and the amazing benefits it brings to the table. In this section, we're diving deep into the world of gamified learning to uncover its effects and explore how it's revolutionizing education.

Now, when it comes to assessing the effectiveness of gamified learning, we've got some key factors to consider. First off, gamified learning puts students in the driver's seat, giving them a sense of autonomy and control over their own learning experience. With progress tracking, achievement badges, and leveling up, students become the heroes of their own learning journey. And guess what? This sense of ownership boosts their engagement and leads to a deeper understanding and retention of the content. Who said learning couldn't be an epic adventure?

Gamified learning is like the ultimate wing man for collaboration and social interaction. Through multiplayer games, team challenges, and friendly leaderboards, students are not just learning solo, they're part of a learning squad. It's all about teamwork, sharing knowledge, and supporting each other's growth. This collaborative spirit not only boosts their interpersonal skills but also creates a classroom vibe that's positive and inclusive. High fives all around!

And here's the cherry on top: immediate feedback, served fresh from the gamified learning kitchen. Games have this magical ability to offer real-time feedback, giving students a chance to assess their progress on the spot. It's like having a personal cheerleader who's got your back. This timely feedback is crucial for students to understand where they shine and where they can level up their skills. Talk about personalized learning at its finest.

Oh, and let's not forget about motivation. Gamified learning knows how to tap into that intrinsic motivation that's hiding in all of us. With a sprinkle of healthy competition, rewards, and recognition, students become unstoppable. They're not just chasing grades; they're fueled by a passion to excel and achieve their goals. It's like igniting a fire within them that keeps burning long after the class ends. Lifelong learners, here they come!

Now, assessing the effectiveness of gamified learning requires some clever methods. We've got the quantitative approach with pre- and post-tests, measuring academic progress and knowledge retention. But let's not stop there. We can also dive into the qualitative side, gathering insights from student surveys, interviews, and classroom observations. It's like getting the full story, capturing student engagement, collaboration, and motivation in action.

Gamified learning is a game-changer in education. By assessing its effectiveness, we unlock its full potential and create dynamic and inclusive learning environments. The autonomy, collaboration, immediate feedback, and intrinsic motivation it brings empower students to become active participants in their own education. The result? Improved academic outcomes and a genuine passion for learning that will carry them through a lifetime of adventure. Game on!

7

Overcoming Challenges and Obstacles

Cracking the Resistance Code: Winning Over Students and Colleagues

Let's face it, incorporating gamified learning strategies can sometimes feel like navigating through a field of resistance. Students and colleagues may be hesitant, skeptical, or just plain resistant to the idea. But fear not, because in this section, we've got some expert advice and techniques to help you address and overcome this reluctance like a pro.

When it comes to students, their resistance can stem from various reasons like fear of change, lack of interest, or doubts about gamified learning's effectiveness. So, how do we break through their walls of resistance? The key is clear and engaging communication. Take the time to explain the advantages of gamified learning in a way that sparks their interest. Show them how it can make learning more enjoyable, boost their motivation and engagement, and ultimately improve their academic performance. Share success stories and real-life examples where gamification has made a positive impact on students' learning outcomes. Paint a vivid picture of how gamified learning can turn their educational journey into an epic adventure.

But that's not all. To truly win them over, get them involved in the decision-making process. Seek their input and feedback through surveys or group discussions. Let them know that their opinions matter and give them a sense of ownership over their own learning experience. When students feel like they have a say in how things are done, resistance tends to melt away like ice cream on a sunny day.

Now, let's tackle the resistance from our esteemed colleagues. It can be trickier since they may lack knowledge or understanding about gamified learning. But fear not, brave educator, because you've got the power to change their minds. Start by sparking conversations about the benefits of gamification and share success stories from other educators who have already embraced gamified learning strategies. Be the shining beacon of knowledge and offer to provide training or workshops to demonstrate effective ways of incorporating gamification into the curriculum. Show them the light, and they'll follow.

Collaboration is key when it comes to addressing resistance from colleagues. Invite them to observe your gamified lessons or share resources and materials that they can use to integrate gamified learning into their own classrooms. Encourage open dialogue and create a supportive environment where teachers can freely express their concerns and challenges. Together, you can conquer any obstacle and find collective solutions to make gamified learning a reality.

And let's not forget the power of ongoing support and resources. Offer professional development opportunities like webinars or workshops, where teachers can learn from experts in the field and exchange best practices. Build a treasure trove of gamification resources, including lesson plans, assessment tools, and game-based platforms, to assist teachers in implementing gamified learning with ease. With the right support and resources, resistance doesn't stand a chance.

Addressing resistance from students and colleagues is no easy task, but armed with effective communication, student involvement, training, collaboration, ongoing support, and a sprinkle of perseverance, you can turn the tides. So, go forth, brave educator, and conquer that resistance. Unlock the power of gamified learning and create an engaging and effective learning environment that will leave resistance in the dust. Adventure awaits!

* * *

Mastering the Art of Time and Resource Juggling in Gamified Learning

Ah, gamified learning, the perfect blend of education and fun. But let's not forget that successful implementation requires some serious time and resource management skills. Fear not, intrepid educators, because in this section, we'll dive into the world of time and resource management for gamified learning.

When it comes to time management, it's all about finding the sweet spot. You want to strike a balance between traditional instruction and the exciting world of game-based activities. It's like trying to bake the perfect cake – too much traditional instruction and the gamified fun gets neglected, too much gamification and the curriculum goals crumble. So, let's whip up a well-planned schedule that allows for both educational content and thrilling gamified experiences. By thoughtfully allocating time, you can create an educational feast that satisfies both your curriculum goals and your students' hunger for gamified learning.

Effective resource management is the secret ingredient to success. Consider the availability and accessibility of technological tools and games that align with your learning objectives. You want to make sure they play nicely with your curriculum and meet the specific needs of your students. Take the time to explore different platforms and tools that offer gamified learning experiences. Evaluate their effectiveness and suitability for your classroom. It's like choosing the perfect spice blend – you want the flavors to complement each other and create a delicious learning experience.

Now, let's sprinkle some collaboration and professional development into the mix. Connect with fellow educators who have mastered the art of gamified learning. Join professional learning communities where you can share experiences, strategies, and resources. Together, you can unlock the secrets of efficient time and resource management. It's like joining forces with a team of master chefs – you learn from their expertise, swap recipes, and create culinary wonders together.

And don't forget to let your students have a taste of responsibility. Involve them in the decision-making process. Give them a voice in selecting games and deciding how to allocate time for gamified activities. When students take an active role in managing time and resources, they develop a sense of ownership over their learning. It's like giving them a seat at the chef's table – they feel valued and empowered.

So, there you have it, the recipe for effective time and resource management in gamified learning. Carefully plan your time, balance your resources, collaborate with other educators, and empower your students. With these skills, you'll create an engaging and effective learning experience that leaves everyone wanting seconds. Bon appétit!

* * *

Navigating the Gamified Learning Maze: Troubleshooting Common Issues

Ah, gamified learning, the land of endless possibilities and engaged students. But wait, even in this fantastical realm, there may be challenges lurking around every corner. Fear not, brave teachers, for in this section, we shall venture forth and conquer the common hurdles that may arise during gamification implementation.

Our first challenge is student disengagement. While gamified learning has the potential to boost motivation, some students may not jump on the gamification bandwagon right away. They may be puzzled by the game mechanics, uninterested in the themes, or simply overwhelmed by the competitive nature of it all. To tackle this, let's sprinkle some personalization into the mix. Allow students to choose avatars or game themes that resonate with their interests. Provide clear instructions and tutorials right from the start, ensuring everyone understands the rules of the game. After all, nobody likes feeling lost in a labyrinth of confusion.

Next up, we face the hurdle of limited resources or technical difficulties. Ah, the technological realm, where dragons of compatibility and glitches await. But fear not, for we have backup plans! If technology is scarce or mischievous, explore alternative options like board games or low-tech game elements that still ignite the spark of gamified learning. Seek the wisdom of the IT department or discover alternative platforms that can slay those technical dragons.

Now, let's navigate the treacherous path of maintaining student motivation and preventing burnout. Ah, the ebb and flow of enthusiasm that can sometimes dwindle over time. But fret not, for we hold the key to renewal! Introduce new challenges, levels, or rewards periodically to keep the game fresh and exciting. Unleash the power of collaboration, where students band together to conquer shared goals. Teamwork makes the dream work, they say.

Last but not least, we face the formidable challenge of assessment and grading. Oh, how traditional grading methods may clash with the gamified realm. But fear not, for we shall forge a new path! Establish clear criteria for earning points or leveling up, guiding students on their quest for success. Provide timely feedback to steer them in the right direction. And hey, let's consider alternative assessment methods, like portfolios or project-based assessments, which can better capture the essence of learning in this gamified adventure.

So, fellow adventurers, as we journey through the realm of gamified learning, let us not fear the challenges that lie ahead. With personalization, resourcefulness, motivation boosts, and innovative assessment, we can conquer any obstacle and create a vibrant and effective gamified learning experience for our students. Onward, to victory!

8

Success is Within Your Reach

Unleashing the Power of Gamified Learning: Real-Life Classroom Adventures

Picture this: a classroom transformed into an exciting realm where learning becomes an epic quest filled with adventure and discovery. Gamified learning has taken the education world by storm, captivating and motivating students like never before. By infusing game elements into the learning process, teachers are creating immersive environments that foster collaboration, critical thinking, and problem-solving skills. In this section, we embark on a journey through practical examples of gamified learning in action, showcasing its remarkable impact on student learning outcomes.

Let's dive into one captivating example: online platforms that offer gamified learning experiences. Imagine a biology class where students step into a virtual laboratory, conducting experiments and exploring scientific concepts in a safe and engaging environment. By earning points, badges, or leveling up, students are enticed to actively participate, diving deeper into the wonders of biology.

Now, prepare for another adventure! Instead of traditional quizzes or exams, teachers are embracing interactive assessments that bring the excitement of games into the classroom. Imagine a history class transformed into a high-stakes game of Jeopardy, where students compete in teams, answering

38

questions about historical events, figures, and concepts. Learning becomes a thrilling competition, fostering teamwork and igniting the fire of healthy rivalry among students.

Gamified learning has even found its way into classroom management and student behavior. Teachers are wielding the power of point-based reward systems or virtual currencies to incentivize positive behavior and create a sense of accomplishment. In a math class, students earn points for active participation, completing assignments on time, and lending a helping hand to peers. These hard-earned points can then be exchanged for small rewards or privileges, transforming the classroom into a motivating haven of positivity.

These real-life examples demonstrate the immense value of gamified learning. By weaving game elements into the fabric of education, teachers are crafting experiences that ignite student motivation, foster collaboration, and sharpen critical thinking skills. Whether it's through online platforms, game-like assessments, or behavior management systems, gamified learning is transforming the educational landscape. So, let's embrace the power of gamification and embark on this exciting adventure together, unlocking a world of engagement and achievement for our students.

* * *

Unlocking the Magic of Gamified Learning: Insights from Teachers and Students

To truly understand the wonders of gamified learning, let's step into the shoes of those who have experienced it firsthand. In this section, we'll dive deep into the heartfelt testimonials of teachers and the enlightening feedback from students, revealing the transformative power of gamification in the classroom.

Teachers who have embraced gamified learning can't help but marvel at the remarkable changes they've witnessed in their students. What was once a sea of disinterest and apathy has been transformed into a lively and engaged group of learners. These teachers have witnessed a surge in student interaction, collaboration, and critical thinking—essential skills for thriving in the modern world.

Take, for example, Mrs. Davis, a high school English teacher and a good friend of mine. She eagerly shares her gamification journey:

"Since I introduced gamified learning in my classroom, it's like stepping into a whole new universe. My students have gone from passive observers to active participants in their own education. With the allure of points, badges, and leaderboards, they eagerly tackle tasks, solve problems, and collaborate like never before. The energy and excitement in my classroom have skyrocketed, and their understanding and retention of the content have improved significantly."

But it's not just the teachers who are singing the praises of gamified learning. Students themselves have voiced their thoughts on the matter, revealing a newfound motivation, empowerment, and investment in their learning journeys. They appreciate the instant feedback provided by gamified platforms, allowing them to track their progress and adjust their strategies accordingly. The element of competition has also added a sprinkle of fun and excitement to their educational adventures.

Let's hear from Maria, a tenth-grade student. She recently shared her experience in a gamified classroom setting:

"I used to dread dragging myself to school in the morning, but now I actually look forward to it. Some days, it feels like I'm stepping into a game or a competition rather than a classroom. We earn points, badges, and compete against other classes—it's a lot more fun than writing notes or doing worksheets. I'm actually learning new things because I'm having fun. I never would have thought English class could be this enjoyable. I still have some classes I'm not crazy about, but the gamified learning has made getting up in the mornings to go to school a whole lot more bearable."

These heartfelt testimonials and insightful student feedback stand as undeniable proof of the positive impact of gamified learning. By infusing game-like elements into the learning process, teachers create an environment that captures students' hearts and minds, fostering active participation, collaboration, and critical thinking. The transformative nature of gamification not only amplifies students' academic achievements but also nurtures a lifelong love for learning.

* * *

Unveiling the Secrets of Successful Gamification: Lessons from the Trenches

In a world where technology evolves faster than you can say "digital revolution," educators face the thrilling challenge of captivating students' attention. Enter gamification—a magical approach that infuses the learning experience with game-like elements, igniting a spark of motivation and propelling students to excel. In this section, let's dive into the insights from successful gamified learning experiences and uncover strategies for implementing them in classrooms to supercharge students' learning outcomes.

Lesson 1: Clear Goals and Objectives:

One of the essential lessons we've learned from successful gamification adventures is the power of setting clear goals and objectives. By giving students a roadmap, a purpose to their learning, we awaken their inner sense of purpose. Gamified learning thrives when it has a defined mission, be it reinforcing content knowledge or nurturing critical thinking skills. When students know where they're headed, they buckle up and stay engaged throughout the learning journey.

Lesson 2: Meaningful Rewards and Feedback:

Another gem we've unearthed is the significance of meaningful rewards and feedback. Gamification thrives on celebrating progress and achievements. But here's the secret sauce—it's crucial to make those rewards meaningful and in sync with the learning objectives. Whether it's badges, leaderboards, virtual currency, or unlocking new levels or content, rewards should light a fire in students' hearts. And let's not forget timely and constructive feedback— students crave that golden nugget of information to track their progress and level up their skills.

Lesson 3: Collaboration and Competition:

Collaboration and competition take center stage in the tales of victorious gamification. By blending teamwork and friendly rivalry, educators unleash a whirlwind of camaraderie and engagement among students. Picture group challenges that make minds meld, cooperative missions that turn classmates into allies, or competitive quizzes that spark a fire in students' eyes. These strategies fuel collaboration, support, and the pursuit of excellence.

Lesson 4: Flexibility and Adaptability:

Flexibility and adaptability are the secret ingredients to success in the realm of gamification. Educators must embrace the art of refinement and adjustment based on student feedback and outcomes. Creating a safe space where students can share their thoughts and suggestions is key. By remaining open-minded and agile, teachers embark on a never-ending quest to improve their gamified learning experiences and meet the ever-evolving needs of their students.

The treasure trove of successful gamification experiences in education reveals invaluable insights that can catapult student engagement and learning outcomes to new heights. With clear goals, meaningful rewards and feedback, collaboration and competition, and a touch of flexibility and adaptability, teachers unlock an extraordinary learning environment that captures students' hearts and minds. Gamified learning is the enchanted key that empowers educators to inspire their students, nurturing a lifelong love for learning and paving the way for remarkable academic achievements.

43

9

Future Trends and Innovations in Gamified Learning

Unleashing the Power of Emerging Technologies: Gamification on the Rise!

In today's fast-paced digital realm, technology has seamlessly woven itself into the fabric of our daily lives. And the realm of education is no exception. While some schools and districts are still dipping their toes into the pool of modern devices and systems, the potential for growth and innovation is boundless. So, let's embark on an exciting journey and explore the untapped potential of emerging technologies and the thrilling gamification opportunities they bring to the table.

Two stars on the technological horizon that hold immense promise for transforming the classroom experience are virtual reality (VR) and augmented reality (AR). These ingenious inventions whisk students away to virtual realms or overlay digital wonders onto the real world, creating interactive and captivating learning experiences. Picture students donning VR headsets to explore ancient historical sites or manipulating AR overlays to conduct mind-boggling science experiments. The possibilities are as vast as the cosmos itself. By harnessing VR and AR, teachers can infuse lessons with a dose of gamification, sparking curiosity, engagement, and unleashing the full potential of critical thinking and creativity.

Now, let's venture into the realm of artificial intelligence (AI), a technological marvel that promises personalized educational experiences. AI-powered platforms are here to dazzle and adapt to the unique needs of each student, offering tailored learning adventures. Teachers, brace yourselves, for you can wield the power of AI to craft gamified learning pathways that unleash customized challenges and rewards, all tailored to students' performance and progress. The result? Boundless motivation and the power to conquer learning gaps with precision and finesse.

Mobile technology has taken center stage, unveiling a treasure trove of possibilities for gamified learning. Mobile apps and games transform the learning experience, empowering students with anytime, anywhere access to educational delights. Teachers, the stage is set for you to incorporate mobile gamified learning platforms, allowing students to embark on their learning odyssey at their own pace. Collaboration and healthy competition await as students embark on thrilling quests, united in their quest for knowledge. And let's not forget the wonders of game-based assessments, where students can showcase their brilliance through interactive quizzes and simulations. The power is in their hands, quite literally!

As torchbearers of knowledge, it is our sacred duty to embrace these emerging technologies and harness the gamification opportunities they bring forth. Let us weave virtual reality, augmented reality, artificial intelligence, and mobile technology into the tapestry of learning, creating immersive, personalized, and awe-inspiring experiences for our students. Gamified learning becomes the catalyst that fuels their motivation and ignites their thirst for knowledge. And as they delve into the realms of gamification, they emerge equipped with the critical 21st-century skills they need to conquer the challenges of the digital age. Fellow educators, the time has come to unleash the power of emerging technologies and embark on a journey where learning and play intertwine. Let the games begin, and let the adventure unfold!

* * *

Embarking on an Adventure with Virtual Reality and Augmented Reality in Education

Note: Before we embark on this exciting journey into the realm of Virtual Reality (VR) and Augmented Reality (AR) in education, it's important to acknowledge that budget constraints can often make acquiring VR and AR gadgets a challenging endeavor for many schools. However, the purpose of this exploration is to inspire and spark ideas that can be adapted to different circumstances. While VR and AR gadgets may not be feasible for everyone, the concepts and principles behind them can still inspire creative solutions that fit within your school's budget. So, let's dive in and discover how we can infuse elements of VR and AR into our classrooms, even if we have to find our own imaginative alternatives. Together, we can unleash the power of gamified learning and create extraordinary educational experiences!

Step right up, ladies and gentlemen, and prepare to have your minds blown by the awe-inspiring wonders of Virtual Reality (VR) and Augmented Reality (AR)! These groundbreaking technologies have taken the world by storm, and education is no exception. Buckle up as we dive into the exciting realm of VR and AR in education, unlocking the doors to immersive and engaging learning experiences like never before.

VR and AR have the power to transport students beyond the confines of the traditional classroom, whisking them away to magical realms where history comes alive, scientific concepts materialize, and imaginary worlds become their playground. With VR, students can witness the wonders of ancient civilizations, explore distant planets, or even shrink down to the size of a molecule. Meanwhile, AR enriches the real world by superimposing digital marvels onto everyday objects, turning textbooks into interactive gateways to knowledge.

The magic of VR and AR lies in their ability to cater to the diverse learning styles and preferences of our students. Visual learners find solace in the immersive, eye-catching landscapes and lifelike experiences that these technologies offer. Meanwhile, kinesthetic learners can jump right in, actively engaging and manipulating virtual objects. By appealing to multiple senses,

VR and AR bring abstract concepts to life and cement them in students' minds.

VR and AR foster collaboration and sharpen problem-solving skills. Picture a virtual world where students join forces to tackle complex challenges, conduct virtual experiments, or unravel mind-bending puzzles. The shared experiences and teamwork in multiplayer VR or collaborative AR environments ignite the spark of critical thinking and camaraderie. And fear not, dear teachers, for you hold the power to provide real-time feedback and guidance as you witness their virtual adventures unfold before your very eyes.

Now, before we strap on our VR headsets and don our AR goggles, let's pause for a moment of reflection. Implementing VR and AR in education requires careful consideration. We must ponder the costs, technical requirements, and ethical implications of their usage. It's vital that we harness these technologies to enhance the learning experience and align them with our curriculum goals, rather than getting lost in the glitz and glamor of novelty.

When VR and AR seamlessly integrate into education, a world of possibilities unfolds before us. These transformative technologies immerse students in captivating experiences, ignite their curiosity, and fuel collaboration. Whether it's a journey to the depths of the ocean or a walk through the annals of history, VR and AR open doors to comprehension, engagement, and exploration like never before.

So, grab your VR headsets, don your AR goggles, and embark on this thrilling adventure into the realm of gamified learning with VR and AR as your trusty companions. Together, let's create an educational environment that inspires, excites, and empowers our students to reach for the stars and achieve their fullest potential.

* * *

The Potential of Gamified Learning for Personalized Education

Gamified learning: the superhero of personalized education! It swoops in, capes flapping, to transform the traditional classroom into an interactive and individualized learning extravaganza. By infusing game elements into the educational experience, teachers become the architects of an engaging and immersive world where students are the heroes of their own learning journeys.

One of the fantastic powers of gamified learning is its ability to adapt and cater to each student's unique needs. No more one-size-fits-all approach! With gamification, teachers can customize content, challenges, and feedback to match the superpowers and progress of each student. It's like having a personal tutor for every student, guiding them through their academic adventures.

Gamified learning brings teamwork and collaboration to center stage. Just like the Avengers joining forces, educational games often include multiplayer features that encourage students to work together towards a common goal. Through collaboration, students learn from one another, developing their communication, critical thinking, and problem-solving skills. It's like a classroom full of superheroes, using their powers collectively to save the day!

And let's not forget the joy factor. Learning should be an exciting roller coaster ride, not a dull and monotonous slog. That's where gamification shines. By tapping into our natural love for challenges, achievements, and rewards, gamified learning transforms education into an amusement park of knowledge. When students are having fun, they become more than passive learners – they become active participants, fully engaged and eager to conquer new educational heights.

Now, let's not get carried away by the superhero hype. Gamified learning is not a magical cure-all. It requires thoughtful planning and implementation. Teachers need to carefully select and design gamified activities that align with learning objectives and curriculum guidelines. And like any good superhero, they must constantly assess their strategies, making tweaks and adjustments as needed to ensure maximum impact.

Unleash the power of gamified learning and let it soar through your classrooms. Embrace the potential for personalized education, where students take charge of their learning, collaborate like superheroes, and find joy in their academic pursuits. With gamification as your trusty sidekick, the future of education is brighter than ever!

10

Reflection and Next Steps

Reflecting on the Impact of Gamified Learning

Gamified learning: the secret ingredient that turns education into an exciting adventure! It's like sprinkling magic dust over the classroom, instantly captivating students and fueling their passion for learning. Let's take a moment to reflect on the incredible impact gamified learning has on our students.

One of the superpowers of gamified learning is its ability to unleash student engagement. By introducing game mechanics like points, badges, and leaderboards, teachers create an environment that is more thrilling than a roller coaster ride. Students are hooked, eager to participate, and compete for the top spot. And guess what? This heightened engagement leads to deeper learning, critical thinking, and a genuine love for acquiring knowledge.

But that's not all. Gamified learning also comes with its own built-in superhero: immediate feedback! With interactive quizzes, simulations, and challenges, students get instant feedback on their performance. It's like having a personal cheerleader by their side, guiding them on their learning journey. Armed with this feedback, students can reflect on their mistakes, make improvements, and unleash their full potential. Talk about a confidence boost!

Let's not forget about the incredible power of collaboration. Gamified learning platforms bring students together like a well-oiled superhero team. They can join forces, tackle challenges, and conquer the world of knowledge together. Through collaboration, students develop essential skills like communication, teamwork, and empathy, preparing them to be real-world superheroes.

And here's the cherry on top: autonomy and choice. Gamified learning puts students in the driver's seat of their education. They get to choose their own learning path, make decisions, and take ownership of their learning experience. It's like giving them a personalized superhero cape that empowers them to explore, create, and conquer any academic challenge that comes their way.

By harnessing the power of gamified learning, we transform the classroom into an epic battleground of knowledge. With heightened engagement, immediate feedback, collaboration, and a sense of autonomy, we create an educational environment where students can unleash their inner superheroes. So, teachers, let's embrace the magic of gamified learning and embark on an extraordinary journey of student growth and success. Together, we can change the world—one game at a time!

* * *

Strategies for Continual Improvement in Gamification

So you've gamified your classroom and the students are loving it. But here's the thing: to keep the momentum going and ensure long-term success, you've got to level up your gamification game. Let's dive into some strategies for continual improvement that will keep the excitement alive!

First up, regular evaluation and feedback. Take a step back and assess how your gamification strategies are working. Are they hitting the mark or falling flat? Seek feedback from your students and colleagues to get a fresh perspective. Their insights can be pure gold and help you fine-tune your approach.

Next, be adaptable and flexible. Just like a skilled gamer adjusts their strategy on the fly, be ready to tweak your gamification techniques. Stay open to incorporating new game mechanics, challenges, or rewards that better align with your learning objectives and student interests. It's all about keeping things fresh and exciting.

Collaboration is key, my friend. Integrate multiplayer game elements that encourage teamwork, communication, and problem-solving. Throw in some group challenges, cooperative quests, or friendly competitions. Not only will it build camaraderie among your students, but it'll also give them the chance to level up their collaboration skills.

Remember, personalization is the name of the game. Customize the gamified learning experience to meet the needs of each student. Let them progress at their own pace, earn rewards based on their achievements, and choose activities that align with their interests. When students have ownership over their learning, they'll be motivated to keep playing and conquering those educational challenges.

And don't forget about your own professional development. Gamification is a dynamic field, always evolving. Stay in the loop by attending workshops, conferences, or online courses that focus on gamified learning. Sharpen those skills and stay ahead of the game.

By implementing these strategies for continual improvement, you'll keep your gamification mojo going strong. Your classroom will be buzzing with engagement, collaboration, and personalization. So get out there, embrace the power of gamification, and let the learning adventure continue!

* * *

Inspiring Teachers to Embrace Gamified Learning

We all know how challenging it can be to capture our students' attention and keep them engaged, but fear not! The power of play and games is here to save the day.

Gamified learning is all about infusing elements of games into our teaching methods to create an immersive and enjoyable learning experience. By tapping into students' natural love for games, we can ignite their curiosity and passion for learning like never before.

One of the remarkable benefits of gamified learning is its ability to foster active participation and collaboration among students. With features like leaderboards, badges, and levels, we can create a fun and healthy dose of competition and teamwork. Not only will this enhance their problem-solving and critical-thinking skills, but it will also empower them to take ownership of their learning journey.

But that's not all! Gamified learning offers immediate feedback, allowing students to track their progress and identify areas where they can level up. By rewarding their accomplishments along the way, we inspire them to keep pushing forward and reaching for the stars.

Now, let's talk about practicality. Implementing gamified learning requires thoughtful planning and design. We'll explore strategies and examples that align with your curriculum and learning objectives. Don't worry, we'll cover digital tools and platforms for all comfort levels, so no one gets left behind.

By embracing gamified learning, we'll create a classroom culture that values creativity, collaboration, and critical thinking. We'll transform our teaching practices and inspire our students to become active, motivated, and lifelong learners. It's an adventure worth taking!

11

Conclusion

As we come to the end of "Game On: Level Up Your Teaching," I hope this journey into the world of gamified learning has sparked your imagination and filled you with excitement. Throughout this book, we have explored the potential of gamification to transform the educational landscape and enhance the learning experience for our students.

We began by delving into the fundamentals of gamification, understanding its core principles and the psychology behind its effectiveness. We discovered that by incorporating game elements into our teaching, we can unlock a world of engagement, motivation, and collaboration within our classrooms.

From designing gamified lessons to implementing effective strategies, we have learned how to create dynamic and immersive learning experiences. We have explored the importance of aligning gamification with curriculum objectives, providing meaningful challenges, and fostering a positive classroom culture that encourages growth and exploration.

We have also explored a wide range of digital tools, platforms, and resources that support gamified learning, understanding that technology can amplify our efforts and offer endless possibilities for creative and interactive experiences. Remember, these tools are not just for students but can also be a source of inspiration and support for us as educators.

Throughout our journey, we have uncovered the numerous benefits of gamified learning. We have witnessed the power of increased student engagement, motivation, collaboration, critical thinking, and academic achievement. We have seen how gamification can tap into students' natural curiosity, transforming the learning process into an adventure filled with joy, discovery, and growth.

Now, as we reach the end, I urge you to take what you have learned and put it into action. Embrace gamified learning as a powerful tool in your teaching arsenal. Take those first steps towards gamifying your lessons, creating immersive experiences, and empowering your students to become active participants in their own education.

Remember, the journey will have its challenges. You may encounter obstacles or face moments of doubt. But with each challenge, there is an opportunity for growth. As educators, we have the power to adapt, iterate, and refine our gamification strategies. We can learn from our students, experiment with new ideas, and continually evolve as we discover what works best for our unique classrooms.

So, my fellow educators, I encourage you to embark on your own gamification journey. Embrace the joy of teaching and learning, infuse your lessons with game-like elements, and watch as your students' enthusiasm soars. Let your creativity run wild, and don't be afraid to take risks. Remember, the greatest rewards often come from stepping outside our comfort zones.

Together, let us transform education and create vibrant, engaging, and meaningful learning experiences. Let us embrace gamified learning as a catalyst for student growth, inspiration, and lifelong love for learning. The power is in your hands. Level up your teaching and let the games begin!

Resources: Getting Started with Gamification

The following are a handful of resources that are great for gamifying learning! I am, by no means, endorsing any particular service, although I've used quite a few of these myself. I am providing this list as a means of helping you get started on your own gamification journey.So, roll up your sleeves and embark on your own exploration to discover resources that will bring fun and engagement into your classroom!

BreakoutEDU.com: If you're looking for educational games and puzzles that will bring excitement to your classroom, BreakoutEDU.com is the place to go. With a wide range of subjects and grade levels covered, this website offers engaging and interactive learning experiences that will leave your students eager for more.

Brainpop.com: Dive into the world of Brainpop.com, where educational games, videos, and quizzes await. Explore various subjects and topics while having fun and expanding your knowledge.

Classcraft.com: Transform your classroom into an epic adventure with Classcraft. This web-based platform empowers students to create their own characters, form teams, and earn points for academic and social skills. Meanwhile, teachers have the tools they need to manage classroom behavior, track student progress, and communicate with parents. It's a win-win for everyone involved!

Classdojo.com: Say hello to Class Dojo, your digital classroom companion. This website allows you to create personalized and engaging classrooms where students can earn points for positive behaviors and skills. With features like feedback sharing, photo and video sharing, and direct messaging with parents, Class Dojo makes it easy to motivate students and foster a collaborative and improved learning environment.

Dreamscape.com: Unleash your imagination with Dreamscape.com. This website lets teachers create captivating games tailored to their students' needs. The games are designed to align with curriculum standards and offer an interactive and enjoyable way for students to learn and practice various skills.

Duolingo.com: Get ready to embark on a language-learning adventure with Duolingo. This app turns language learning into a game, where you earn points, level up, and unlock new skills. With bite-sized lessons and a focus on speaking, listening, reading, and writing, Duolingo makes language learning fun and addictive.

Edulastic.com: Looking for interactive and engaging assessments? Look no further than Edulastic.com. This platform empowers teachers to create assessments that captivate students and make learning come alive.

Kahoot.com: Prepare for some interactive and fast-paced fun with Kahoot!. This website lets you create and play quizzes, polls, and surveys in real time. Whether you're in the classroom or remote, Kahoot! enhances learning and engagement. Join live games hosted by others or challenge yourself with solo play.

Quizizz.com: Say goodbye to boring quizzes and hello to Quizizz.com. This website adds a playful twist to learning by allowing educators to create and play interactive quizzes with their students. It's a great tool for gamifying the learning experience, motivating students to participate, compete, and have a blast while learning.

Quizlet.com: Flashcards and memorization just got a whole lot more enjoyable with Quizlet. This website offers a variety of interactive games, flashcards, and tests to help you study different subjects. Join study groups, compete with other learners, and take your learning to the next level.

Socrative.com: Looking to spice up your classroom with interactive quizzes, polls, and games? Socrative.com has got you covered. Engage your students in friendly competition, provide instant feedback, and reward their progress with this web-based platform designed to gamify learning.

There's a whole world of resources out there that I haven't even touched upon. The beauty of gamifying your classroom is that you get to shape your own vision and discover the tools that perfectly fit your teaching style and your students' needs. It's time to dive in and start exploring. Experiment, tinker, and find what works best for you. And when you find that resource that aligns with your goals and makes your gamified learning experience even better, you'll know you've hit the jackpot.

So go ahead, have a blast, and let the gamification adventure begin!

About the Author

Hi, my name is John. I'm a middle school math and literature teacher with over a decade of experience making learning fun and engaging for my students. If you are anything like me, you're always looking for ways to better engage your students and add more zest to your lessons.

Back in 2016 I stumbled onto something called "gamification", before I knew it had a name. My teaching had become routine...aka "boring". I realized that making learning more game-like, with points, levels, challenges, etc. hooked students into the lessons. The students were so much more engaged, motivated, and yes, learning more too!

When I'm not teaching or writing, you can usually find me enjoying time spent with my beautiful and supportive wife, our fun-loving daughters, and our two rambunctious dogs.

You can connect with me on:

🌐 https://www.jriggs.net

Subscribe to my newsletter:

✉ https://onlyawanderer.medium.com

Also by John Riggs

Author John Riggs draws from his 10+ years of experience revamping his own elementary and middle school classes with gamification. His work guides you step-by-step through concepts like rewards, competition, storytelling, and technology integration to create interactive, game-inspired learning environments.

Play to Learn

Ready to transform your classroom into a dynamic and engaging space where learning is not just a task, but an exciting adventure? "Play to Learn: Increase Student Outcomes Through Meaningful Play" is the key to unlocking the full potential of your students and revolutionizing your teaching approach.

Ideal for both beginners and experienced educators, "Play to Learn" is an invaluable resource for anyone looking to enhance their teaching techniques. Don't miss out on this opportunity to reshape the future of education, one game at a time. Get your copy now before the price changes!